How to Find

Best Clients on the Internet

summary

Introduction

Finding the most valuable customers on the internet can seem like something out of this world…

but it is not!

When you understand the right mechanisms, the subtle approach and what your routines are like, the client appears as if you were the **only solution for him**.

Everything is linked to your communication, your delivery and how much value you generate.

Understand who your ideal customer profile is and understand their needs and expectations, so you can deliver efficient solutions and gain the trust of the most valuable consumers on the market.

And it is precisely with the intention of helping you in this search that I created this material, so that you can gain the confidence necessary to approach your dream clients.

With the information and strategies in this material, you will be able to stand out in the market and achieve the success you have always dreamed of. So, get ready to explore the full potential of your business and win the best customers!

Identifying the ideal customer

Identifying the profile of the ideal customer is essential for any business that seeks to offer efficient solutions and achieve success in its sales strategies.

It is necessary to understand the needs and expectations of the target audience in order to meet demands satisfactorily and gain consumer loyalty.

To begin identifying the ideal customer profile, it is important to define the market niche in which the business operates.

Based on this, it is possible to analyze consumer behavior, their characteristics, desires and preferences, as well as the main trends and opportunities in the sector.

Another relevant aspect is the collection of data and information through surveys, questionnaires, interviews and data analysis. These tools allow you to identify consumer patterns and behaviors, in addition to understanding what they expect from a product or service.

By knowing the profile of the ideal customer, it becomes easier to develop targeted marketing, communication and sales strategies that meet consumers' needs and expectations in an assertive and efficient way.

Furthermore, it is possible to improve the products or services offered, adding value and standing out from the competition.

Another important point is maintaining a close relationship with customers, listening to their suggestions and criticisms and constantly seeking to improve the consumer experience with the brand. This helps to build public loyalty and create a virtuous cycle of referrals and recommendations.

Using psychographic questions

to find the ideal client

Psychographic questions seek to understand an individual's behavioral, personality traits, values and interests.

They help to build a more complete profile of the target audience for a product or service, going beyond demographic characteristics, such as age, gender and geographic location.

Psychographic questions explore the motivations, desires and needs of the target audience, allowing the company to develop a more efficient strategy to communicate with them and offer solutions that meet their expectations.

These questions can be asked in market research, interviews, questionnaires and other types of direct approaches to the target audience. It is important that they are open-ended questions, which allow the respondent to give more complete and honest answers, without limiting them to pre-defined options.

Psychographic questions are a valuable tool for understanding the behavior of the target audience and defining the ideal customer, allowing the company to develop more efficient strategies to win and retain its customers.

30 psychographic questions to understand your target audience

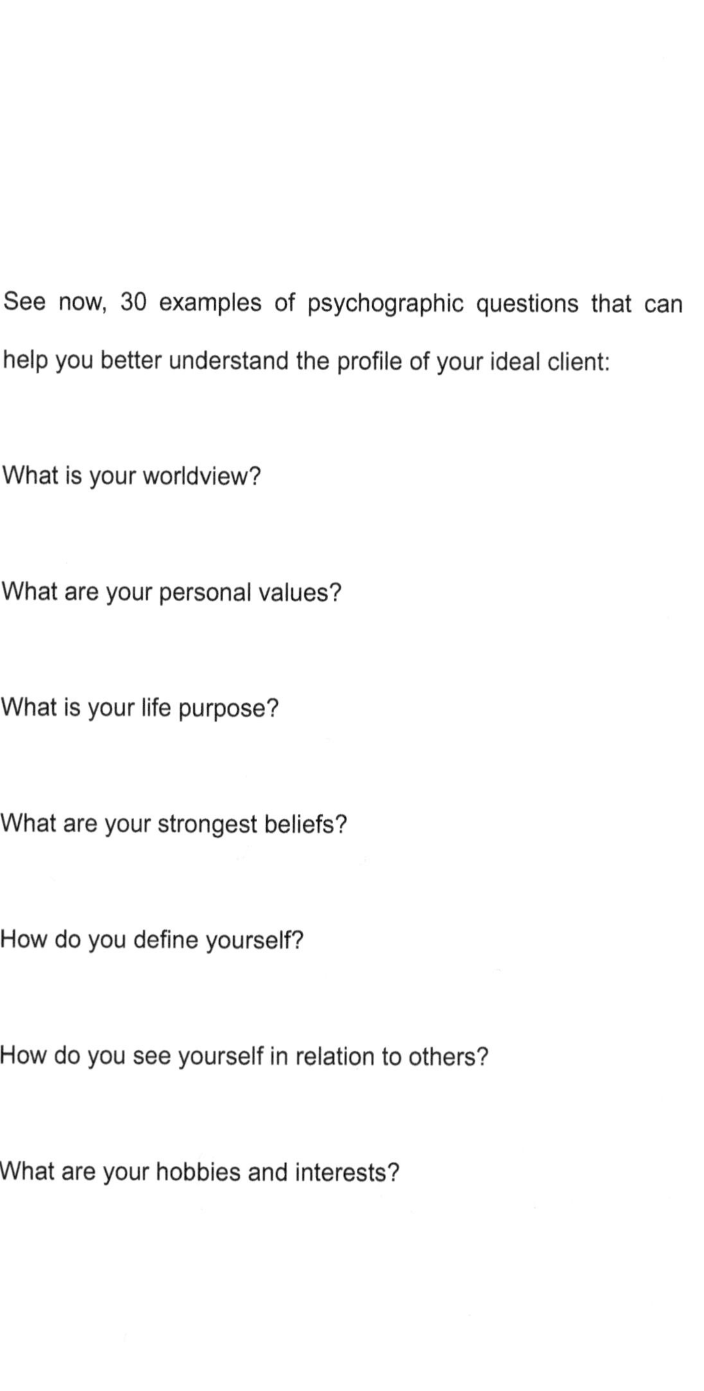

See now, 30 examples of psychographic questions that can help you better understand the profile of your ideal client:

What is your worldview?

What are your personal values?

What is your life purpose?

What are your strongest beliefs?

How do you define yourself?

How do you see yourself in relation to others?

What are your hobbies and interests?

How do you relate to technology?

How do you consume information?

How do you make decisions?

What is your level of self-knowledge?

How do you deal with your emotions?

How do you relate to family and friends?

How do you deal with pressure and stress?

How do you feel about your work?

How do you feel about money?

How do you feel about health?

How do you feel about happiness?

How do you feel about spirituality?

How do you feel about love?

How do you feel about education?

How do you feel about the culture?

How do you feel about politics?

How do you feel about religion?

How do you feel about justice?

How do you feel about freedom?

How do you feel about the environment?

How do you feel about technology?

How do you feel about fashion?

How do you feel about food?

These questions can help you better understand your target audience's interests, desires, values, and beliefs, which is essential to creating an effective marketing strategy.

Remember that not all questions are relevant to all types of business and that it is important to adapt them according to your segment and objective.

How to find the best customers

on the internet

Finding potential customers on the internet can be a challenging task, but there are several ways to identify and attract potential buyers.

Some of the main strategies are:

Advertise on social networks, such as Facebook, Instagram and LinkedIn;

Make use of strategic keywords on your website and blog to increase visibility in search engines;

Participate in discussion groups on social networks related to your market niche;

Produce relevant content and share it on your social networks and blog;

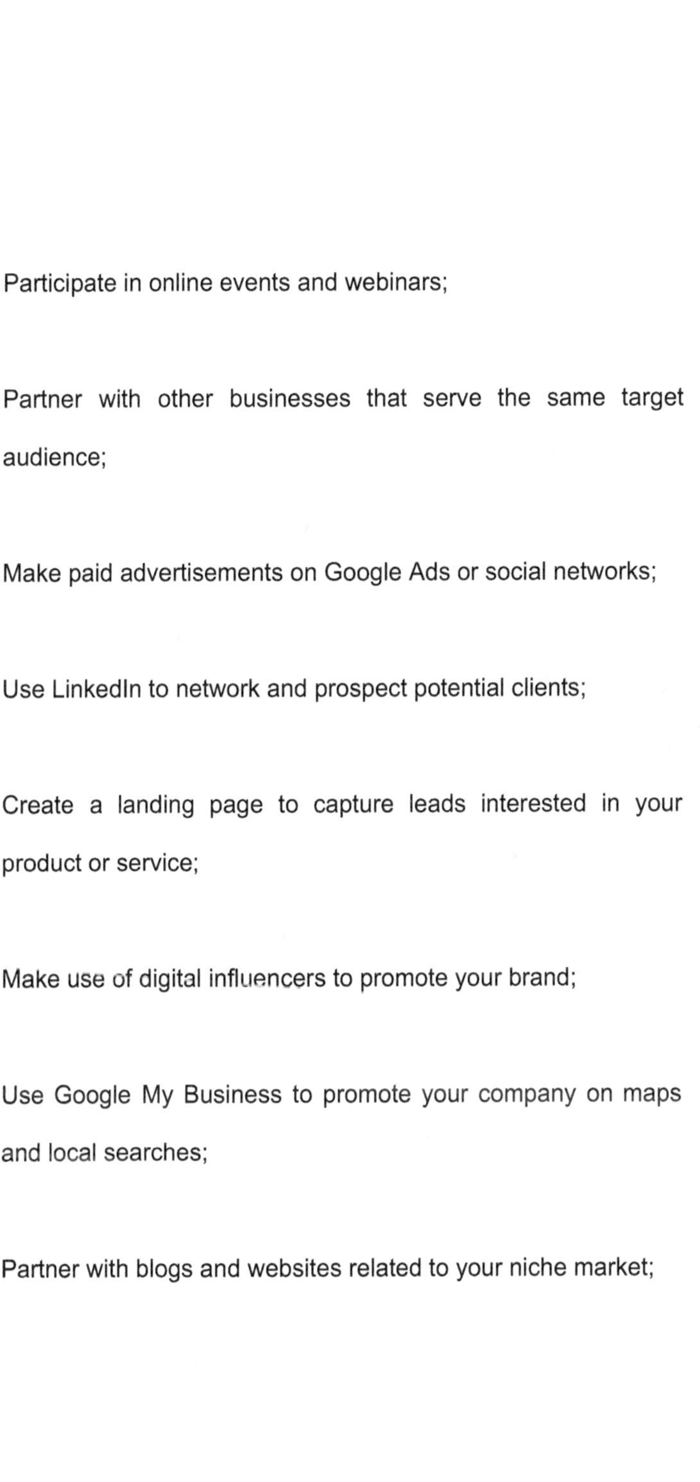

Participate in online events and webinars;

Partner with other businesses that serve the same target audience;

Make paid advertisements on Google Ads or social networks;

Use LinkedIn to network and prospect potential clients;

Create a landing page to capture leads interested in your product or service;

Make use of digital influencers to promote your brand;

Use Google My Business to promote your company on maps and local searches;

Partner with blogs and websites related to your niche market;

Make use of marketing automation tools to generate leads;

Use Google Analytics to monitor traffic on your website and identify opportunities for improvement;

Make use of videos to present your product or service;

Use Pinterest to promote your product or service through images;

Participate in online forums related to your niche market;

Make advertisements on podcasts related to your market niche;

Use TikTok to promote your product or service through short, creative videos.

Social networks have become a powerful tool for connecting people and companies around the world. In each of them, it is possible to find a wide variety of profiles and interests, which makes it possible to discover experts and potential clients in an efficient and creative way.

When browsing social media, it is possible to find groups and communities of people who share the same interests and goals. This way, you can connect with people who have needs and desires similar to those that your business offers, creating a base of potential customers who can be impacted by the solutions you offer.

In addition, social networks also offer a variety of tools that allow segmentation and profile analysis, making it possible to find experts and potential customers according to their interests and online behaviors.

With this, it is possible to create more personalized and targeted approaches, increasing the chance of success in converting these contacts into real customers.

But for this to happen, you must always be attentive and constantly search for new connections.

Social media offers many opportunities to find and connect with experts and potential clients, but you need to invest time and energy in this search to get the results you want.

Therefore, if you are looking to find your dream client, social media is an excellent option. Invest in research, seek to connect with relevant people and companies in your niche, participate in groups and communities, ask questions and offer personalized solutions. With dedication and strategy, it is possible to find the ideal customers and transform them into great business partners.

Instagram + 2 billion active users

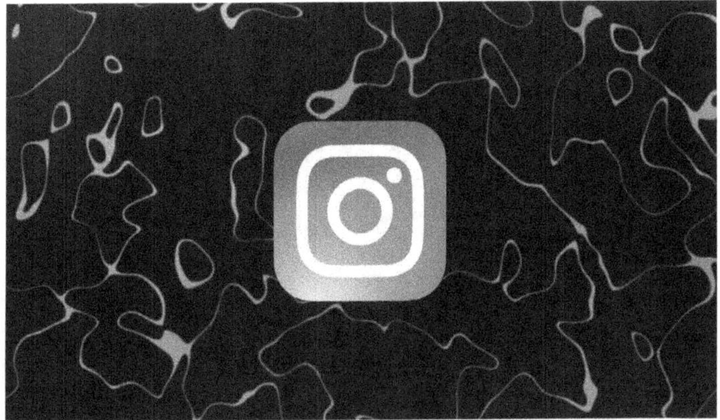

Instagram is one of the most used social networks in the world, and it is a great platform for those who want to carry out market research and find potential customers.

See a step-by-step guide on how to search on Instagram using hashtags and explore:

Define your search terms: Start by defining the terms you want to search for, such as keywords related to your niche market or industry.

Access the search tab: tap the magnifying glass icon in the bottom corner of the screen to access the Instagram search tab.

Select the "tags" option: within the search tab, select the "tags" option and enter the keywords you want to search.

Explore other options: In addition to hashtags, you can explore other options in the search tab, such as the "explore" tab.

In this option, Instagram displays suggestions for posts, profiles and hashtags based on your interests and behaviors on the social network.

Analyze the results: After performing the search, analyze the results and explore the posts, profiles and hashtags related to your search terms.

Seek to identify potential customers and experts on the subject, and interact with them through comments, likes and direct messages.

Use analysis tools: to improve your searches, you can use hashtag and profile analysis tools, which allow you to identify user metrics and behaviors related to your search terms.

By following these steps, you can perform efficient searches on Instagram and find potential clients and experts on the subject. Remember to interact in a genuine and personalized way, offering solutions relevant to your contacts' needs.

Using hashtags to your advantage

Hashtags are an important tool on Instagram for finding new customers and connecting with people who are interested in your product or service. By using the right hashtags, you can increase your profile's visibility and reach a larger audience.

To use hashtags on Instagram to find customers, follow these steps:

Identify relevant hashtags: Research which hashtags are most used in your niche market. This can include hashtags related to your area of expertise, your product or service, or even the interests of your target audience.

Add hashtags to your post: When creating a post on Instagram, add relevant hashtags in the caption or comments.

It is important not to exaggerate the number of hashtags used, as this can harm the quality of your post.

Search relevant hashtags: Use relevant hashtags to find potential customers.

Research the hashtags your target audience typically interacts with and join the conversations taking place on those hashtags.

Follow users who use these hashtags: When you find interesting users who use the relevant hashtags, follow them to build a relationship and become visible to them.

Interact with users who use these hashtags: Comment and like posts from users who use the relevant hashtags.

This interaction can generate new business opportunities and increase the visibility of your profile.

By using hashtags on Instagram strategically, you can increase your profile visibility, find new potential customers, and grow your business efficiently.

For example, a therapist can use hashtags on Instagram to find potential clients who are interested in her services and increase the visibility of her profile.

Some examples of how a therapist can use hashtags correctly include:

#behavioral therapy, #family therapy, #clinical psychology, among others. She can also use hashtags related to the problems she deals with, such as #anxiety, #depression, #relationships, among others.

Remember, it's important to use relevant hashtags and interact with users who use them to get the best results.

How to approach people on the internet

Approaching people you don't know on the internet can be a challenge, especially if you are looking to make sales or establish business partnerships. However, there are some practices that can help you approach these people efficiently and respectfully.

One of the first things you can do is research the person you want to approach.

Search for information on social networks, websites and blogs, and try to understand what her interests and goals are. This way, you can adapt your approach and create a more assertive connection.

Another strategy is to seek to establish a relationship of trust before approaching the person directly with a business offer.

This can be done through comments on publications, sharing relevant content and engaging in groups of common interests.

When approaching the person directly, it is important to be respectful and clear about your objective. Be polite and avoid being invasive or aggressive in communication. It is also important that the offer you are presenting is relevant to the person, and not just an attempt to sell at any cost.

It is important to remember that not everyone will be willing to receive a commercial approach on the internet. Respect the person's right to not be interested and don't pressure them to change their mind. The approach must always be based on a relationship of respect and mutual interest.

Asking questions to understand a person's personal and professional goals can be an efficient strategy to create a more assertive approach and offer solutions relevant to their needs.

Below, I will show you some questions that can help in this process:

What are your main personal and professional goals at the moment?

What do you hope to achieve in the short and long term?

What are the main difficulties you face in your personal or professional life?

How do you define success in your personal and professional life?

What do you believe you need to develop or improve to achieve your goals?

How do you deal with changes?

What are your main interests and hobbies?

What do you look for in a business partner or a company you work for?

When the person answers these questions, you will have some insights to develop the conversation and create a strong connection with that customer.

How to approach professionals on

Linkedin

Having an approach script on LinkedIn is a great way to communicate with other professionals and start conversations more efficiently and assertively. However, it is important to remember that the script should serve as a guide, not a formula.inflexible.

Each person is unique, and you need to adapt your approach depending on the situation and the person you are communicating with. Furthermore, it is important to personalize the message and show genuine interest in the contact's profile.

Therefore, it is important to have a well-structured approach script as a starting point, but always be open to adaptations and variations when communicating on LinkedIn. This way, you will be able to create more authentic and lasting connections on the social network.

See some models below that are very assertive in their approach.

Hello [person's name],

I saw that you work in the area [name of area] and I was very interested in your trajectory and experience in this area. I would like to connect with you and exchange some ideas about the trends and challenges in this market.

Additionally, I would like to know more about your current work and if you have any tips for someone just starting out in the field.

I believe we can exchange a lot of valuable information and who knows, even collaborate on a project in the future.

I await your response and thank you in advance for your attention.

Yours sincerely,

[Your name]

Hello [person's name],

I really liked your profile and your professional experiences. I realized that we have some things in common and I believe we could talk about some ideas I have in mind.

I'm looking for people with an innovative and creative outlook, and I believe you may have the vision I need to develop new projects.

I would like to know if you are open to talking more about your experiences and professional goals, and if possible, we could schedule a virtual coffee to exchange ideas.

I await your response and thank you in advance for your attention.

Yours sincerely,

[Your name]

Hello [person's name],

I was browsing LinkedIn and ended up coming across your profile. I was impressed by your experience and results achieved, especially in the area of [area name].

I work with [your area of expertise] and I believe we could exchange valuable information and even find some synergy between our areas of expertise.

I'd like to know if you're available for a quick chat so I can learn more about your experiences and current projects.

I await your response and thank you in advance for your attention.

Yours sincerely,

[Your name]

How to find customers on YouTube

YouTube is a video sharing platform that can be an excellent tool for finding potential customers. To find your ideal customers on YouTube, follow the steps below:

Identify your target audience: Before you start looking for customers on YouTube, it's important to have a clear idea of your target audience. For example, if you are a business coach, your target audience could be entrepreneurs and business owners.

Search for relevant channels: Do a YouTube search for channels that are relevant to your target audience. For example, if you are a business coach, look for channels related to business and entrepreneurship.

Interact with users: Watch channel videos and interact with users through comments. Answer questions, offer your opinion, and show interest in their problems and concerns.

Create your own channel: Create your own YouTube channel and produce content relevant to your target audience. Make sure to include relevant keywords in your video titles and descriptions.

Use YouTube ads: YouTube offers ads to help promote your videos and reach a larger audience. You can use targeted ads to reach a specific audience based on their age, location, and interests.

Create a call-to-action: In your videos, encourage viewers to subscribe to your channel, visit your website, or contact you for more information.

By following these steps, you can use YouTube to find potential customers and promote your business efficiently.

Remember, it's important to provide valuable, relevant content to your target audience and engage with users to establish a relationship and build trust.

How to prospect companies on Google

There are several efficient ways to prospect companies on Google and approach them correctly.

Keyword research: Use keywords relevant to your business and look for companies that could benefit from your services.

Business Directories: There are several business directories available on the internet. Use these lists to find companies that meet your ideal customer profile.

Social media: Many companies have an active presence on social media. Use LinkedIn, Facebook and other networks to find companies and connect with key people within them.

Ads: Create ads on Google Ads that target companies that could benefit from your services. Make sure your ad is relevant and appealing to your target audience.

Participation in events: Participate in events related to your market niche. These events are great opportunities to meet other companies and key people within them.

When approaching companies, make sure you have a message that is personalized and relevant to each one. Demonstrate that you understand the company's specific needs and how your services can help them achieve their goals. Remember that the goal is to build a lasting relationship with the company, so stay focused on the value you can offer them.

Mistakes that keep you from finding your ideal clients

There are several mistakes that can alienate a business from its customers, but below are the most common mistakes that should be avoided:

Lack of communication: Lack of communication is one of the most common mistakes that keeps a business away from its customers. If you don't communicate clearly and frequently with your customers, they may feel ignored and look for other options in the market.

Lack of attention to needs: Another common mistake is not paying attention to the customer's needs. If you don't offer products or services that meet your customers' needs, they may look for other options in the market.

Lack of quality service: Quality service is essential to keep customers satisfied and loyal to your business. If you don't offer quality service, customers may feel undervalued.

Lack of innovation: Lack of innovation can cause your products or services to become obsolete or outdated compared to the competition. It is important to stay up to date with market trends and invest in new technologies and ideas to offer innovative solutions to your customers.

Lack of commitment: It is important to show commitment to your customers by offering adequate support and assistance when required and ensuring customer satisfaction in all aspects.

The importance of follow-up in prospecting

Follow-up is one of the most important parts of the prospecting process. Often, the people you approach are not ready to make an immediate decision, either due to lack of time or resources. However, that doesn't mean they aren't interested in your offer. This is why it is essential to carry out adequate follow-up to ensure that you maintain the relationship with the potential client and can eventually close the deal.

But what is follow-up?

Follow-up is the action of keeping in touch with a potential customer after the first interaction. This interaction may have occurred through a phone call, an email, a message on social media or any other means of communication. The goal of follow-up is to keep the prospect interested in your offer and eventually make a sale.

This strategy is important because most people don't close deals right away. In fact, most deals close after several interactions. This is because people often need time to think and analyze their options before making a decision.

By following up, you are reminding the prospect of your offer and demonstrating your interest in helping them. This helps build trust and credibility, which is essential for making a sale.

Additionally, follow-up helps ensure you don't miss business opportunities. Sometimes a potential customer may be interested in your offer but may have forgotten to respond or may have been interrupted by other obligations. By following up, you are staying in front of the prospect and ensuring they don't forget about you.

30D method

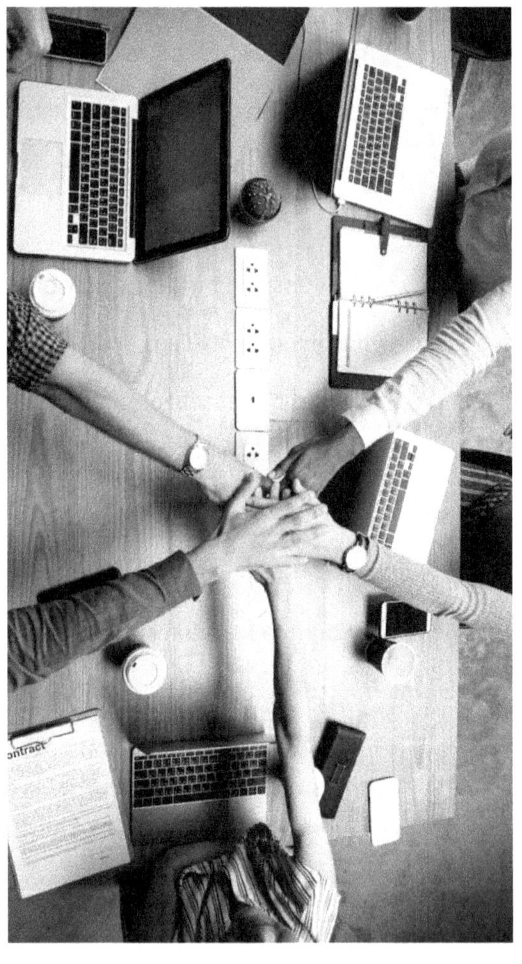

The 30D Prospecting Method is a strategy that consists of approaching at least 10 people per day for 30 days, showing interest in helping them with your services or solutions. The idea behind this method is to create a consistent and systematic prospecting habit, which will result in positive results in the long term.

The first step to implementing the 30D Method is to clearly define your target audience and what your prospecting objectives are. With this information in mind, you can identify people who are potential customers and approach them with a personalized and targeted message.

During the first few days of the method, you may encounter some resistance or even rejection. However, it is important not to get discouraged and continue to focus on your goal of approaching one person per day. Over time, you will develop communication and persuasion skills that will help you become more effective at prospecting.

Over the 30 days, it is important to keep a record of all approaches that were made, as well as all conversations that were initiated. This will allow you to assess what's working and what's not, and make adjustments to your approach based on the results you get.

Finally, it is important to remember that the 30D Prospecting Method is a long-term strategy, which requires consistency and persistence. Although the results may not be immediate, if you maintain discipline and determination, the results will definitely come. There is no way to resist a sincere approach and an interest in helping, especially when the offer is targeted at the specific needs of the potential customer.

So, if you want to increase your conversion rate and ensure a steady flow of new business, the 30D Prospecting Method is the right strategy for you. Remember that success in prospecting depends mainly on consistency and persistence, so stay focused and keep moving forward!

Relationship funnel with social media messaging

It is worth remembering that this funnel is just a suggestion and can be adapted according to the needs of your business.

First contact: At this stage, you must seek to establish a connection with the potential client.

A good way to start this conversation is with a brief, personalized message, mentioning a common point you have.

For example: "Hello, I noticed that you are also a fan of *Tedx*! What's your favorite?"

Breaking down objections: It is common for potential customers to have some objections before closing a deal.

At this stage, you must anticipate these objections and work to minimize them. One way to do this is through messages that reinforce the benefits of your product/service and answer possible customer questions.

For example: "I understand you may have some doubts about the effectiveness of our product, but keep in mind that it has already been tested and approved by many satisfied customers."

Social proof: Here, you should use messages that show the success and satisfaction of other customers. This can be done through testimonials, success stories or even through referrals from old customers. For example: "See what some of our customers are saying about our company..."

Offer: At this stage, you must present an irresistible offer to the customer, which encourages them to close the deal.

One way to do this is through messages that highlight the value that the customer will receive when purchasing your product/service.

For example: "Don't miss the opportunity to achieve your goals with our product! Now, for a limited time, we are offering a special discount for new customers."

Closing: Here, you must use messages that encourage the potential customer to make a decision and close the deal. It is important to remember that, even at this stage, you must maintain a respectful and personalized approach, taking into account the customer's needs and preferences.

For example: "I'm here to help you with any questions or concerns that may arise. What do you think about starting right now to achieve your goals together?"

Remember that the relationship funnel is not a linear process and the potential customer can contact you at any of these stages. The important thing is to maintain clear and objective communication, focused on the customer's needs, and work to earn their trust over time.

Creating a commercial proposal

impossible to ignore

A commercial proposal is essential for winning new business and closing contracts.

I will present you with an infallible structure to help you create a successful commercial proposal:

Know the client: Before preparing a proposal, it is important to understand the needs and expectations of your potential client.

Do some research on the company and the person you will be communicating with. This will help you personalize the proposal and increase the chances of success.

Define the objectives: It is important to be clear about what your proposal wants to achieve. Define the objectives you hope to achieve with your potential client, such as increasing sales, reducing costs or improving performance.

Offer specific solutions: In the proposal, highlight the solutions you can offer to solve the customer's problems. Be clear and objective, presenting the advantages and benefits of your offer.

Present the differences: It is important to highlight the differences between your company and its competitors. Show what makes your company unique and what advantage this will bring to the customer.

Define the value: In the proposal, present the value of the service or product you are offering and justify the price. Show how your offer is a good investment for the customer.

Show credibility: Present your company's success stories and testimonials from satisfied customers. This will help increase the credibility of your proposal and the client's trust.

Include a call-to-action: Finally, include a call to action in the proposal, inviting the customer to close a deal or get in touch for more information.

Remember that a well-crafted commercial proposal can be the difference between closing a contract or not. Dedicate time and effort to create a personalized and efficient proposal for your ideal client.

Conclusion

Throughout this material, you learned several strategies for finding and winning over your ideal client.

Through the use of psychographic questions, hashtags on social media, approach scripts and relationship funnel, you will have an easier time identifying the needs and expectations of your target audience.

We know that finding your dream client can be a challenge, but with the techniques presented in this material, you will have the necessary tools to stand out in the market and win the most valuable clients.

Remember that, in addition to applying these strategies, it is important to have persistence and creativity when approaching potential customers.

Constant practice and analysis of the results obtained will help you improve your selling skills and become an increasingly successful professional.

Take advantage of all the knowledge acquired and put it into practice as quickly as possible.

We are confident that you will achieve your goals and gain the freedom and confidence necessary to approach the most valuable customers on the market.

Success!